GW00726895

FIGHTS

OF

FANCY

First hardback edition printed 2014 in the United Kingdom

A catalogue record for this book is available from the British Library.

ISBN 978-0-9928859-2-2

Published by

For more copies of this book, please email: contact@beyondthrilled.com

Printed in Great Britain

FIGHTS OF FANCY

STEVE REDSHAW AND RICHARD PENDRY

MADE UP TEAR UPS,
FIGHTS OF FANCY,
IMPROBABLY DOUBTFUL BOUTS.

WHO'S GOT THE WIT FOR
THESE FAR FETCHED
CONFLICTS?

AND WHO'LL WIN
WITH A GRIN
WHEN IT COUNTS?

IF A POTATO KNEW KARATE
AND A HALIBUT HAD FISTS

WHO WOULD END UP
BATTERING WHO?

AND WHO'D HAVE
HAD THEIR CHIPS?

DARTH VADER
AGAINST SHAKESPEARE!

LIGHT SABRE VERSES QUILL!

WOULD THE DARK LORD
GET RUFFED UP?

OR COULD HE TAKE DOWN
BILL AT WILL?

WOULD A HEN PECKED
FIGHTING COCK BE SHOCKED

WHEN BOXED BY A
KANGAROO?

OR WOULD THE ROO CHICKEN OUT
WHEN PUNCHED IN THE POUCH

AND BID THE ROOSTER COCK
TOODLE-OO?

IF A STRIKING PYROMANIAC
AND A SMOULDERING
ARSONIST CLASHED

WOULD THEY GET ON LIKE
A HOUSE ON FIRE?

OR WOULD EACH ONE
MEET THEIR MATCH?

SO HOT!

COULD A TRUMPED UP
JACK OF CLUBS

BEAT DOWN THE
ACE OF SPADES?

OR WOULD THE SHOVEL
WIELDING ONE DIG DEEP

AND SEND THE BRAVE
KNAVE TO HIS GRAVE?

IF A COCKATOO
COULD VOODOO

AND A BEAGLE
GOT THE NEEDLE

WHO'D END UP
PINNING WHO DOWN?

AND WHO'D WIND UP WITH
A PUNCTURED EGO?

COULD OPPENHEIMER'S BOMB
KILL THE FUTURE
WITH ONE BLAST?

OR WOULD
HIGGS' BOSON PARTICLE
ATOMISE THE PAST?

WHEN A PIRATE
CAPTAIN'S PARROT

SETS UPON THE
SHIP'S FIRST MATE,

WHAT'S THE PECKING
ORDER THEN?

WHO ENDS UP IN
PIECES OF EIGHT?

IF A VINTNER SPILT
A BREWER'S PINT

WOULD A CORKING
BATTLE RESULT?

OR WOULD A QUICK BOP
WHILST CAUGHT ON THE HOP

SEE THE BREWER LOSE HIS
BOTTLE AND BOLT?

WOULD A SABRE TOOTHED
TIGER BE RATTLED

BY A DENTIST
WITH A SINISTER GRIN?

IF HE BIT THE DRILL DOWN
WOULD THE CAT
WEAR THE CROWN?

OR BE FOILED
AND GET FILLED IN?

WOULD A CENTIPEDE COBBLER
END UP SIX FEET UNDER

IF HE BOOTED HIS
WELL HEELED RIVAL?

WHO'D NAIL THEIR FOE
AS THEY WENT TOE TO TOE?

AND WHO'D BE THE
SOLE SURVIVOR?

IF AN EXTRA STRONG MINT
WITH A STEELY GLINT

GOT TASTY WITH
A BIRDS EYE CHILLI

WHO'D STAY COOL WHEN
THINGS GOT HOT?

AND WHO'D END UP
LOOKING SILLY?

WHO'D CRACK FIRST,
THE CHICKEN OR THE EGG,

IF ONE HATCHED A PLOT
AGAINST THE OTHER?

WOULD THE CHICKEN RUN
WHEN THE SHELLING BEGUN,

OR WOULD THE BATTERY
CAUSE THE HEN NO BOTHER?

IF A MYOPIC
GOGGLE EYED TROGLODYTE

TRIPS UP A
TYRANNOSAURUS REX

THE NEANDERTHAL
NEED NOT WORRY AT ALL

NO DINO HITS A
BLOKE IN SPECS!

BUT REMEMBER...

THE PEN IS MIGHTIER
THAN THE SWORD
AS A NOBLE MAN ONCE SAID.

SO IF YOU FANCY A FIGHT,
BE QUICK ON THE DRAW,

NOT WITH A BLADE,
BUT A PENCIL INSTEAD!

Lightning Source UK Ltd.
Milton Keynes UK
UKIC01n2223110714
235002UK00002B/2